Economic Coordination in the European Economic Community

CONRAD J. OORT

Program in International Business
Graduate School of Business Administration
The University of Michigan
Ann Arbor, Michigan

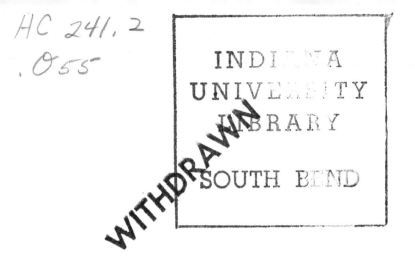
Copyright © 1967
by
The University of Michigan

A Publication of the
Bureau of Business Research
Graduate School of Business Administration
The University of Michigan
Ann Arbor, Michigan

Printed in the United States of America

PROGRAM IN INTERNATIONAL BUSINESS

Since 1961 the Graduate School of Business Administration of the University of Michigan has conducted a Program in International Business, made possible originally by a Ford Foundation grant to the University to support international studies in various fields. The chief use of the funds allocated to this School has been to enlarge the teaching program, with the aim of fulfilling the growing need for competent and informed persons to direct business operations abroad. It has also been possible to carry on a wider range of research and publication on questions related to foreign commerce. Results of the research are published in the *International Business Studies* series. Publications currently included in this series are listed below.

The Balance of Payments and Domestic Prosperity, by Paul W. McCracken and Emile Benoit, No. 1, 1963.

Leading World Stock Exchanges, by Wilford J. Eiteman and David K. Eiteman, No. 2, 1964.

Capital Markets of the European Economic Community, by Antonin Basch, No. 3, 1965.

Educating Asian Students for Business Careers, by James D. Scott, No. 4, 1966.

Management of International Advertising: The Role of Advertising Agencies, by Gordon E. Miracle, No. 5, 1966.

The Doctor, the Hospital, and the Patient in England: Rights and Responsibilities under National Health Service, by Arthur F. Southwick, Jr., No. 6, 1966.

Stock Exchanges in Latin America, by David K. Eiteman, No. 7, 1966.

Inflation and Development in Latin America: A Case History of Inflation and Stabilization in Bolivia, by George Jackson Eder, No. 8, 1967.

Economic Coordination in the European Economic Community, by Conrad J. Oort, No. 9, 1967.

FOREWORD

Every country in the European Economic Community is individually committed to certain major short-term economic policy objectives (full employment, balance of payments equilibrium, and price level stability) as well as to some form of medium-term national economic planning. The Community as a whole is also concerned with these objectives. Because of the growing interdependence of the nations in the Community, no single nation can pursue its individual economic objectives without profound and immediate repercussions from its partners. There are important potential conflicts of interest between the nations of the Community and the Community as a whole. These conflicts can be resolved only by the formulation of a common policy, or at least some form of policy coordination.

As a simple illustration, we may consider a nation that is confronted with a balance of payments problem. The traditional procedure might be to restrict home demand, devalue the currency, or restrict trade in payments with its partners. However, in the integrated European Economic Community, committed to a free movement of goods and services, any of these steps would have an immediate and highly disruptive impact on the partners and would present serious problems to the Community. In short, the ability of an individual nation to pursue its economic objectives at the expense of its partners is severely limited, and it is therefore necessary to develop policies that will promote these objectives on a Community-wide basis.

This monograph deals with the problems of coordinating and integrating economic policy and planning in the European Economic Community. Professor Oort analyzes the present situation and discusses the outlook for policy coordination within the Community in the specific areas of exchange rate adjustments in the common currency, capital flows, income policies, and medium-term national economic planning. The book is a slightly expanded version of a series of three public lectures given by Professor Oort while he was Visiting Professor at the University of Michigan Graduate School of Business Administration during the 1966-67 academic year. The

Visiting Professorship is sponsored jointly by the Dutch govern-
ment and the University of Michigan in honor of the Dutch settlers
in Michigan as a means of promoting international understanding.
The Program in International Business is pleased to make Professor
Oort's keen analysis of the problems of the European Economic
Community available to a wider audience.

Robert W. Adams, Director
Program in International Business

Ann Arbor, Michigan
September, 1967

CONTENTS

I

TOWARD A COMMON CURRENCY

In its 1962 Action Program, the European Commission stated that "the establishment of a monetary union could become the objective of the third stage towards the Common Market." At the present time, well into the third stage of the transitional period of the Common Market, this statement seems overly ambitious and perhaps even unrealistic. For monetary union implies a full transfer of national monetary authority to a common institution, comparable to the Federal Reserve Board in the United States.

But this in turn implies an almost complete loss of national autonomy by the individual countries in the entire area of stabilization policy. This is so because the European countries, somewhat disenchanted with the technical and political potentialities of effective fiscal policies for combating inflation, have relied to a large extent on monetary measures to regulate their economies in the short run. Moreover, monetary union implies a unified capital market and consequently the unrestricted access of one country's fiscal authorities to the capital markets of the entire Community. Since there is no effective market check on the borrowing power of governments—the threat of bankruptcy being totally unrealistic —one government could, in a unified capital market, drain off short-term as well as long-term funds from other countries and thus not only contravene the economic policies of these other countries but also effectively determine the monetary situation in the entire Community. Since this is obviously unacceptable, monetary union implies a Community-imposed restriction on the borrowing power of individual governments, thus severely limiting their freedom of action with regard to fiscal policy as well.

Unification of capital markets, monetary union, and a common macroeconomic policy are really all different sides of the same die. No single one of them can exist without the others. Effective unification of capital markets implies not only the elimination of a great number of still existing legal, administrative, and fiscal barriers to the free and undistorted movement of capital across

national boundaries, but it also and primarily implies an unconditional exchange and convertibility guarantee for the different national currencies. This is equivalent to a monetary union; and, as I
have just mentioned, it requires common monetary and fiscal policies as a necessary complement.

These few comments must suffice to give you a first indication
of the immense problems that stand in the way of full monetary
union. The European Commission, in its 1962 Action Program,
squarely faced the issues involved when it stated as a precondition
for monetary union "the establishment of one single center for
economic policy, . . . national policies being eventually merged into one." All this again sounds somewhat unrealistic at the present
time because it requires a surrender of national autonomy in the
areas which are closest to the very heart of national economic
sovereignty: the power to tax and to spend (historic prerogative of
national states and the power base of parliament in a democratic
society), the management of money, and, last but not least, the
delicate and very complex issues associated with a national incomes policy. In a community of nations which has virtually
halted all major progress towards establishing the institutional and
political conditions for meaningful common action, which is gradually eroding the power of the federal institutions and has never
granted any to its federal parliament, even discussing monetary
union would seem decidedly Utopian at the present time.

In view of this, it may be well to ponder very briefly the down-
to-earth issues involved, the real grass-roots economic importance
of monetary union. It has been said by someone who can hardly
be accused of excessive and unrealistic idealism, "L'Europe se fera
par la monnaie, ou elle ne se fera pas"; Europe will be created by a
common currency or she will not be created at all. For it is evident
that full monetary union is a necessary precondition for the emergence of the true European corporation, which is discussed in
Chapter II. As long as monetary union and all that it implies in
terms of common policies is not achieved, there remains a risk of
exchange rate variation and, far more seriously, of the reimposition of exchange restrictions or barriers to the free movement of
goods, services, and capital within the Community. No firm will
allow itself to become too vulnerable to this latent threat by completely integrating the operations of different plants situated in
different countries of the community. This will tend to preserve

the national bias in the Common Market's industrial structure and rob the economic integration of its real economic payoff.

But enough has been said about the fundamental importance of the final goal of common policies in this area. For the time being, our objective must be far less ambitious and our efforts must, perforce, concentrate on ways to achieve the minimum of policy coordination necessary to implement and preserve the essentials of the Common Market: namely, the free movement of goods and services, of labor and, as far as possible, of capital. The real questions are these: What should be done? How can it be done, given the Treaty of Rome and the present political climate? What has, in fact, been achieved so far?

Let me begin by eliminating one aspect of policy coordination that is exceedingly important in practice but not really specifically relevant to the European Economic Community. It is the aspect of consultation between member states on the policies to be carried out by each of them. Mutual information on policy intentions is extremely important and becomes more so as the economic interdependence of the six nations increases. The policies pursued by a country's partners in the Community will have an increasingly strong impact on its own economy and therefore become an ever more important parameter in its own policy decisions. There is also an important learning process involved when policy makers with experience of different situations and different national solutions get together regularly. Finally, mutual exchange of information on policy creates within the national administration a sort of pressure group consisting of high officials who are dedicated to achieving something in the area of policy coordination in which they are so actively engaged, often for a very long time.

This type of regular policy consultation has been extremely important in the postwar world; witness, for example, the cooperation in the area of international liquidity and the various rescue operations of the pound sterling. But it is hardly the specific prerogative or achievement of the EEC. In fact, the broader international organizations, such as the IMF and the Organization for Economic Cooperation and Development, are more appropriate forums, from the point of view of information and learning. The OECD, in particular, has exploited the intergovernmental approach for all it is worth. The procedure of country examinations has been effective in creating a maximum of pressure towards coordination of policies with a minimum of formal powers.

In the European Economic Community, consultations on macroeconomic policy have taken place primarily in the Monetary Committee, which consists of high national officials responsible for monetary policy in their home countries, and in the Committee on Stabilization Policy, which is likewise made up of highly placed civil servants of the EEC countries. In these committees, the six countries have engaged in regular consultation: the committees have made frequent recommendations for economic policies to be followed by the member countries. This process of consultation, persuasion, and mutual learning has not been without influence. The Monetary Committee, for example, has recommended the introduction of minimum reserve ratios as an instrument of monetary policy in France, a recommendation that has been carried out successfully. The repeated warnings of the Monetary Committee and the Committee on Stabilization Policy about the inflationary pressures in the Community have undoubtedly strengthened the hand of national governments, or of finance ministers within the national governments, in their struggle against the continued pressures for more expenditure and lower taxes.

All this is not unimpressive. But if the European Economic Community wishes to justify its separate efforts, it must go beyond the stage of mere consultation, which I shall therefore leave out of discussion.

It may seem that I am thus eliminating practically everything that EEC has done in the field of common stabilization policy. For the achievements of the Community to date are really no more, when boiled down to hard facts, than consultation in the various committees just mentioned, leading to informal recommendations to member states and Community institutions and, since 1964, involving yearly formal recommendations directed by the Community to the member governments on the macroeconomic policies to be followed by the states. These recommendations, incidentally, do register a certain progress, in that they reflect a consensus on the immediate concrete objectives of macroeconomic policy and the means by which they are to be achieved. The first of the so-called "Marjolin recommendations," for example, set a concrete limit of 5 per cent on the increase of public expenditure and recommended an incomes policy directed at a parallel development of nominal per capita income and the trend of per capita growth of the real national product.

But these are only recommendations, which need not be and in fact have not been carried out by member governments. Moreover, although the Treaty of Rome is not quite clear as to whether these recommendations must be accepted by unanimous consent, they have in actual fact been tacitly assumed to be subject to the unanimity rule. Consequently, no government need accept a recommendation which it does not want; and, once a recommendation has been accepted, a government need not carry it out, since there is neither legally nor practically any way of enforcing it. When all is said and done, one might well ask whether all this is not really just an elaborate facade, with practically nothing behind it other than, again, consultation and persuasion.

This picture may be somewhat overpessimistic, if it is interpreted as portraying the potential for effective common policies under the Rome Treaty. The carrots and the sticks which the Treaty does provide have not been put to the test, essentially because of the excessive U.S. balance of payments deficits and the corresponding surpluses of the Six.

I cannot go into the intricate problem of defining what is excessive in terms of the world's need for international liquidity. Nor do I want to make any predictions about future developments, except to state the obvious fact that the extent to which the United States can continue to run excess deficits is limited by its gold reserves. When these have been run down to the danger point, action will have to be taken to stop the excessive deficits one way or another. Whether autonomous market forces will have solved the problem before drastic action becomes inevitable is largely a matter of conjecture, but the changed price relationships between the United States and Western Europe lead me to think that powerful economic forces are in fact operating under the surface to reverse once more the pendulum's direction in the curious postwar swing from dollar shortage to dollar glut and back again, which was firmly believed by almost everyone to be a permanent feature of the economic scene. Let me just mention one figure in this context. During the last six years the price index of manufactures has risen approximately two and a half times as fast in the Common Market as it has in the United States. Moreover, the volume of U.S. investments in the Common Market may well taper off when the rush to beat the EEC tariff wall is no longer powerfully reinforced by the comparatively high profitability of investment in the Common Market. Despite all criticism of the profit motive as a short-term determinant of investment behavior, it surely is highly operative when considered in the somewhat longer perspective.

Whatever comes of this, the European euphoria caused by plentiful reserves will end sooner or later and restore the effectiveness of balance of payments constraints on the European economies. When that happens, the Treaty provisions, which were supposed to induce policy coordination, will get a chance to become effective, as they have not been in the past.

For only in a situation in which the international liquidity positions of individual countries are threatened by balance of payments deficits does the Community impose real constraints on a country's freedom to carry out whatever national policies it wishes to pursue. In those circumstances, and only in those circumstances, there may be a real conflict between autonomous policies and obligations under the Treaty of Rome. And, surely, the Community means something in terms of macroeconomic policy only if it does in fact impose policies that would not have been carried out voluntarily otherwise.

The constraints imposed by the Treaty are really rather severe. For it is the general tenet of the Rome Treaty that a country is prohibited from unilaterally reimposing restrictions of any kind on trade or payments within the Community. Moreover, the freedom of trade and payments within the Community automatically makes any unilateral restrictions with respect to third countries entirely pointless. Imports or money transfers that cannot be effectuated directly can always be achieved via other members of the Community. Consequently, any restrictions, whether within the Common Market or outside it, can be imposed only by common decision of the member countries. Potentially, this is an extremely strong federal element in macroeconomic policy, even though it happens to have been ineffective in the past years because of the reserve euphoria. A Common Market country that gets itself into balance of payments difficulties appears to have only two major options: either to deflate its internal economy, i.e., to accept the rules of monetary and fiscal discipline that are the real content of monetary union, or to turn to the Community, which by common action under Article 108 of the Treaty may grant assistance or authorize the reimposition of certain restrictions, both under conditions to be established by the Community.

In other words, either a country behaves voluntarily in a

manner consistent with the ultimate goal of monetary union, or it is forced into a situation in which the conditions for an effective common policy are satisfied.

The system looks almost airtight in theory, given the additional fact that unilateral action in defiance of the Treaty is virtually impossible without seceding from the Community (which, by the way, is not legally possible either). The obligation not to impose unauthorized restrictions is law in the Community and can be enforced by any interested party in court. In this sense, the European Economic Community is a community of law and basically different from such arrangements as the European Free Trade Association, where obligations can be enforced only by retaliation—a device which, if used, may fatally weaken the free trade zone by undermining the confidence of the business world in its permanence.

To what extent is the EEC system, as I have just described it in these all too brief and general terms, a sufficient framework for effective common policy? Or, in other words, do we need any positive common policies over and above the negative policy coordination which consists in the prohibition of unilateral restrictions, with escape clauses supervised by the Community? Cannot macroeconomic policy be left to the national states, to be carried out within this framework of Community-supervised constraints?

Community documents appear to imply that positive policy coordination is necessary because the freedom of interstate trade and payments makes countries progressively more sensitive to disturbances in the economies of their partners, while at the same time their defensive weapons such as import and exchange restrictions have been outlawed. Every country therefore has a vital interest in the macroeconomic policy carried out by its partners, an interest that should be reflected, it is implied, in policy's being made on the community level rather than nationally. These facts themselves are not in dispute, but the reasoning, although rather convincing at first sight, is not really decisive. Coordination, after all, can be brought about by common rules of the game as well as by common discretionary action. If this were not true, decentralization of decisions would never be possible, and the much maligned invisible hand of the market mechanism would have to be abandoned completely and in all economic affairs. For, as the trite and overworked saying goes, everything in economic affairs depends on everything else. The real reasons for positive policy coordination, if any, must be found in more specific shortcomings of the system of rules, with the Community-supervised exceptions that I have just outlined.

One obvious gap in the system of the Rome Treaty concerns exchange rates. Exchange rate variation is neither outlawed nor subjected to common decisions. The Treaty only mentions piously that "each member state shall treat its policy with regard to exchange rates as a matter of common interest." It has been argued, although as far as I know exclusively by academic economists, that freely fluctuating exchange rates, possibly within certain limits that would be substantially larger than those imposed by the IMF rules, could reconcile autonomous national macroeconomic policies with the abandonment of all authority to impose restrictions on trade or payments. I cannot go into the complex issues raised by the general question of free versus fixed or pegged exchange rates, nor do they seem to be particularly relevant to the situation in the EEC. A system of floating exchange rates would appear to be exactly the reverse of what is desirable. Instead of moving toward a stronger discipline imposed on the individual countries' monetary and fiscal policies, necessary as a first step to monetary union, the system of free exchange rates tends to weaken that discipline by opening up an autonomous or a nationally manipulated escape, namely, exchange rate variation. Moreover, exchange rate variation is hardly conducive to a real integration of the national markets, since, as I have said before, no firm can really integrate the operations of its separate plants in different states if national currencies are subject to exchange variations. Every businessman, every banker, and every policy-maker that I know of agrees completely on this point. The recent elaborate Community report on the unification of capital markets does, in fact, recommend not a widening but a narrowing of the limits of exchange rate variation for the currencies of the Six. Apparently, the money illusion in our economic system is such that it is far easier to live with changes in relative prices than with changes in exchange rates, even if the latter would tend to offset the former, and even though more and more contracts are being tied to some kind of price index.

In any case, the Community appears de facto to be moving toward a system of mutually pegged exchange rates with a Community procedure for possible adjustment. On a formal level, little has been done beyond stipulating prior consultation in the case of intended exchange rate variation. But as a matter of practical policy unilateral exchange rate variation is clearly inconsistent with the system of agricultural subsidies based for some major products on a common price, defined in the Community's common unit of account. A unilateral devaluation, for example, would raise the grain price in terms of national currency, possibly inducing an increase in production, which would automatically increase the disbursements from the common agricultural fund and thus impose a real additional burden on the other countries of the Community. This would clearly be unacceptable, unless the devaluation were agreed upon by the partners.

This brings me to another area, that of the external policies of the Community. In its relations to other countries the Community has a real choice between internal adjustment, exchange rate variation with respect to other currencies, and imposing restrictions. Imposing restrictions on trade or payments, as I have said before, is necessarily a matter of common policy on account of the absence of internal barriers and the resulting ineffectiveness of unilateral restrictions towards other countries. Given a system of virtually fixed exchange rates within the Community, the same would hold for exchange rate variation. The resulting need for positive policy coordination with respect to the outside countries does not really conflict with the procedure of negative policy coordination I have just outlined for the Community's internal relations in this area. Balance of payments difficulties of the Community as a whole are necessarily reflected in balance of payments difficulties of individual countries, which will then either deflate (and thus solve the problem for themselves as well as the Community without explicit common action) or apply for assistance or exchange rates adjustment, which automatically carries the problem to the Community level.

There may, of course, be another way open to the individual country—namely, turning to international institutions for assistance—which would permit it to escape both the discipline of the balance of payments constraint and the resort to Community action. The Community has attempted to bring this recourse within its confines by adopting a decision that consultation shall take place before a country takes any such steps. This obligation is not very strict, and it has in fact been flagrantly disobeyed, in particular by Italy when that country obtained substantial short-term credits from the International Monetary Fund and the United

States during its balance of payments crisis a few years ago. But this escape from Community discipline is really only of limited importance. At some point, a country facing balance of payments problems will still have either to deflate or to apply for Community action in the field of exchange rate adjustment, restrictions, or assistance. Consequently, the logic of the system necessarily and automatically implies a common external policy of the Community.

So far then, the system appears to have no major logical loopholes. But there still remains the more important question: Will it work in practice, and will it work satisfactorily? I want to take up this question first on its technical economic merits and then look at the political viability of the system.

It has been said that the system of negative policy coordination necessarily contains a deflationary bias, since the burden of the adjustment tends to be placed primarily on the deficit country. I am not particularly impressed with the general argument. In fact, on the level of generalities there is everything to be said for this so-called bias. If it is true that countries tend to expand to the limit of their resources, there is an obvious need for some kind of constraint and for an adjustment process that puts the burden on those who have exceeded the constraint. The penalty itself, then, of deflation may be painful and from a purely abstract economic point of view wasteful, but it is in reality an essential preventive check to overexpansion, a check which can be weakened only at the price of permanent and universal inflation. In Western Europe, my generation has grown up in a climate of virtually permanent inflationary pressures. We have for more than twenty years experienced the strong inflationary bias inherent in our present political and economic system, which, fortunately, has shed the many pre-Keynesian taboos, such as balanced public budgets, that inhibited a rational approach to macroeconomic problems. But in doing so we have loosened the reins and given the system a very obvious and strong inflationary bias. Under those circumstances a somewhat rigid balance of payments constraint may not be a bad thing at all. Provided the growth of world liquidity keeps pace with the need for additional international reserves, associated with the expansion of international trade, there is no reason that I can see why a more rigid discipline within the Community would not be a very welcome offset to the inflationary bias in the political make-up of our countries.

The real issue is whether, given the present volume and growth of international reserves and the present tools of economic policy, which exclude unilateral restrictions, the system permits a continued expansion at high but not excessively high levels of employment, without frequently running into balance of payments deficits of a magnitude that cannot be financed from the reserves.

I realize that this statement is exceedingly vague. For one thing, the definition of a high but not excessively high level of employment depends on several structural elements in the economy—the absence or presence of regional problems, as in southern Italy, and of major structural shifts such as the coal crisis in Belgium, etc.— and it is also to some extent a matter of social choice. Not long ago, for example, we in the Netherlands considered a level of unemployment of around 2½ to 3 per cent of the labor force as a workable norm of policy; after almost seven years of experience with an unemployment level of less than ½ of 1 per cent we have become conditioned to much higher levels of employment. Although ½ per cent is considered excessive by all, including the labor movement, and is in fact now in the process of being redressed, a return to the norm of 2½ to 3 per cent is extremely unlikely to be politically acceptable.

Although for all these reasons it may be difficult, if not logically impossible, to determine whether the present level of international liquid reserves would be sufficient to enable countries to run their economies at an acceptable average level of employment, one thing is certain. The establishment of the Common Market will tend to increase the amplitude of individual balance of payments deficits and surpluses among the Six, for the simple reason that the individual economies become much more open to their partners. Already, the share of intra-Community trade in the Community's total GNP has almost doubled since 1958, and it will undoubtedly increase further as the process of economic integration progresses. Any disturbance either in the home economy or in the economy of the partner countries will be reflected to a much larger degree than before in the balance of payments of individual countries.

The consequences of this development are very familiar to anyone who has been associated with economic policy in a highly open economy, such as that of the Netherlands. With a marginal propensity to import of well over 50 per cent, anything is reflected immediately in the balance of payments. The balance of payments in that situation becomes a major signal variable of economic policy, even though this has been pushed somewhat into the background in the last eight years because of the excessive U.S. balance of payments deficits, which have made internal containment of inflation, rather than balance of payments equilibrium, the number one economic policy goal.

My provisional conclusion is that the establishment of the Common Market will substantially increase the amount of international reserves necessary for each individual country if it is to run its economy at a high level of employment without frequent recourse to escape clauses. With a return to more normal developments in the creation of international dollar reserves, the EEC countries would therefore have to devise a procedure for substantial mutual lending.

I should like to draw your attention, however, to three counter-tendencies which make the problem somewhat less dramatic than it might seem at first sight.

1. The fact that home inflation spills over to the other countries, which eases the adjustment by forcing some of the inflation on the surplus countries in the Community. In a relatively small group with a high proportion of internal trade—almost 50 per cent of total international trade of the Six is intra-Community—this effect will tend to be relatively important and to increase in importance as economic interdependence increases. I may mention, however, that in the recent past the cycles of the EEC countries have been markedly out of phase. The reasons for this would merit a separate discussion for which there is, unfortunately, no space. But the fact does indicate that the cyclical spillover within the Community operates with a substantial time lag, which in turn implies that, for the near future at least, intercountry balances of payments may continue to show fairly large fluctuations.

2. The various countries' increased propensities to import, a result of their becoming more open with respect to trade with the Community partners, also make adjustment to balance of payments problems relatively easy, since both the price and the income effect which internal restrictions of demand have on a country's exports and imports will tend to increase. On balance, the problem of keeping within the limits of given international liquid reserves will probably still be larger than it would have been without the Common Market, but not so much greater as might appear at first sight. Moreover, it may be politically somewhat

easier to contain internal overexpansion, since this will show up faster and more dramatically than it used to in the balance of payments.

3. The gradual freeing of capital movements between the member countries may also ease the adjustment by inducing short-term or long-term capital flows between surplus and deficit countries within the Community.

   As long as full monetary union has not been achieved, this third factor ·of increased freedom of capital movement will be of limited importance. Neither the private sector of the economy nor the banking system will be willing to hold large amounts of foreign debt, since such foreign debt will continue to carry an exchange and convertibility risk that will increase as foreign holdings increase. This is as it should be, because in the absence of monetary union, unlimited monetization or quasi-monetization of foreign debt would mean that the balance of payments discipline is robbed of all immediate relevance to policy, with nothing to replace it as a ceiling on national expansionary ambitions.

This last point hits on the essential problem as well as the paradox of the situation.

On the other hand, once capital movements are substantially free and the capital markets become fully communicating vessels, the automatic credits available to an individual country become excessive. A country can simply raise money in the markets of the other member states, either directly by floating loans in these other markets or indirectly by slightly tightening the home market and thus inducing a flow of funds to it. In effect, this would mean that one country has automatic access to any other member country's international reserves, without any effective check. This is obviously unacceptable.

There is therefore a double problem. Initially the problem is to increase the insufficient international reserves of the member countries. As capital movements are liberalized, however, the problem changes into a need for monetary and fiscal discipline to replace the vanishing discipline of the balance of payments.

The obvious answer to this double problem is to marry the difficulty of insufficient reserves in the initial period to the increased need for policy coordination as the freedom of capital movements progresses. This would imply that what we need as a first step is decidedly *not* the extension of automatic or semiautomatic interbank credits between countries, as foreseen in many of the ingenious schemes that have been thought up to increase international liquidity. Automatic or semiautomatic credits are precisely what we do *not* want, since they make no contribution whatever to the essential issue: moving toward coordination of monetary and fiscal policies. In fact, the automatic extension of credits makes such a development far more difficult. Instead, the initially increased pressure of the balance of payments discipline would appear to present a golden opportunity to force the countries of the Common Market into a monetary and fiscal discipline, which is the necessary complement of monetary union. It provides the one chance to make the system of negative policy coordination an effective tool towards positive coordination.

The procedure that is explicitly foreseen in the Treaty is not adequate in this respect. Member states may be asked to grant credit to a country experiencing balance of payments difficulties, but they are under no obligation whatever to accede to the request. The institutional and legal basis is far too weak either to insure regular credit operations where such are really needed or to develop an effective and permanent policy coordination. What would be needed is a permanent credit basis, established by a partial pooling of the international reserves of the member countries. The technical aspects of such a scheme are not very complicated, and they have been widely discussed in the past. They would involve the creation of an EEC Reserve Fund, in which each country would be obliged to hold a fixed percentage of its international liquid reserves.

In most proposals that have been made, the Fund would extend automatic or semiautomatic credit up to a certain margin above its basic quota, much as in the present International Monetary Fund system. However, if the EEC Reserve Fund is to serve as a basis for a development toward monetary unification, it must refrain from all automatic or semiautomatic credit creation. For if it did not refrain it would throw away the one chance to use the increased reserve requirements of the Common Market countries as a lever to bring about an effective policy coordination. Moreover, the EEC Reserve Fund would then have no real reason for a separate existence, next to such institutions as the International Monetary Fund and the European Monetary Union. If the proposed EEC Reserve Fund is to act as a first step toward monetary union, it will have to impose strong and explicit policy conditions under which countries can obtain any credit at all.

Turning to the political aspect, it is of course highly unlikely, at least in the near future, that the EEC countries would be willing to grant extensive powers in this area to an independent Community institution. On the other hand, a procedure of granting such conditional credits by common consent would be inadequate, as long as national objectives still dominate over the interests of the Community at large. For a procedure of common consent involves a risk either of noncooperation between member states in cases where, objectively speaking, credit should be granted or, perhaps more realistically, the granting of credit without strong policy conditions, since countries may be afraid to limit the national autonomy of others, knowing that they themselves may get into a comparable position later on. Moreover, the system of mutual consent throws the granting of credit open to all sorts of horse trading which cannot but weaken the discipline of the credit system.

But it is not inconceivable that the countries of the Common Market might agree on a procedure according to which the granting of credit, up to a certain limit, of course, would be delegated to an independent Community institution, which would operate under the following rules:

1. It would grant unconditional credit to a country experiencing balance of payments difficulties, if the rate of unemployment of that country exceeded a certain structural norm to be determined.

2. If unemployment in the country appealing for credit falls short of this norm, credit can be granted only under the condition that the country asking for credit submit itself to certain policy constraints, the broad lines of which would have been previously laid down in a general "code of good behavior."

3. The Community institution could refuse to give credit at all, but in that case the country would have the right to appeal to the representatives of the national states, who would decide by qualified majority.

I have no time to work out these general ideas, but I just want to mention a few points before passing to the real problem of this proposal, the definition of a "code of good behavior."

One point is that the procedure would have to be integrated with the coordination of external policies. The total application for credit exceeding a certain danger point may, for example, trigger a procedure under which the European Commission would have to propose common action either in the form of tightening the conditions under which credit is to be granted, thus inducing tighter monetary and fiscal policies of the individual countries, or in the form of devaluation of all Community currencies, imposition of restrictions toward other countries, recourse to the International Monetary Fund, etc.

Just one comment about the quantitative significance of an EEC Reserve Fund. If the individual countries of the Community were to deposit 25 per cent of their liquid international reserves with the Fund, this would give the Fund a credit base of some $5 billion, or slightly less than the total present liquid reserves of the largest Community member. A figure of 25 per cent is surely not excessive, considering that almost half of the Community's total trade is within the Common Market.

But, as I have said, the real problem of this proposal is the definition of a "code of good behavior." Such a code would have to deal primarily with fiscal policy, because there is no doubt that the major internal source of inflationary pressures in Western Europe and elsewhere has been the public sector.

A general norm of good fiscal behavior could be defined in terms of the "structural budget deficit or surplus," sometimes referred to in Europe as the "Zijlstra norm," after the Dutch Finance Minister who has actively advocated it for some time as a general norm for budgetary policy. Its basic concept is the structural difference between private savings and private investment at full employment. Public expenditures and tax rates should be set so that the budget shows a deficit or a surplus just sufficient to bridge the structural gap between private savings and investments at full employment. The norm is, of course, very close to the Council of Economic Advisers' concept of a balanced full employment budget, except that the Zijlstra norm leaves room for a structural deficit or surplus.

In practice, the norm operates somewhat as follows. If we start from a base year in which the economy is at full employment equilibrium, the structural norm permits an increase of public expenditure or a reduction of tax rates, with an aggregate expenditure effect equal to the structural growth of GNP multiplied by the overall marginal progression factor of tax rates. There are many possible variations on this theme. One could, for example, require the net expenditure of the public sector to rise by no more than the structural real growth of GNP, regardless of whether the base year is a situation of macroeconomic equilibrium or not. This would still have a countercyclical effect, to the extent that inflationary price increases will squeeze public expenditures. In no version is the norm fully compensating, but experience shows that such an expectation would be highly unrealistic in any case. We would already have made an immense step forward if the government sector were prevented from acting as a source of inflation, as it surely has been in Western Europe.

Similar long-term norms have been proposed and can be worked out for monetary policy. One norm that has been proposed is that the quantity of money should be increased no faster than the liquidity requirements connected with the real growth—structural or actual—of GNP. This is a very strict requirement because it implies that the Central Bank should not finance any rise of the price level. It would not be possible as a consistent policy, but it might be workable as a temporary anti-inflationary device, to be imposed as a condition for obtaining credit from the EEC Reserve Fund if the applying country is experiencing an internal inflation.

These norms would, of course, have to be elaborated and adapted to the situation in each particular country. This is possible only in a longer-term framework. But a workable code of good behavior would have to be a matter of long-term planning in any case, if the institution responsible for running the EEC Reserve Fund and implementing the policies associated with it is to be given an operational basis on which it can carry out its credit policies. Such a code cannot change from year to year, because that would mean giving extensive discretionary powers to the Community institution, for which the countries are simply not yet ready, or it would involve regular decisions by the states by common consent, which might completely immobilize the Fund or weaken its effectiveness in forging common policies. This longer-term framework is discussed in Chapter III.

The yearly recommendations on general economic policy, to be directed at the individual countries, would still have a definite function in this system. They need not be a simple elaboration of the structural norm, worked out for the specific situation of every individual country at that particular time, because the structural norms are only a *ceiling* to be applied when an inflating country applies for credit. But the fact that the Community institution has the power, within the terms of its mandate, to refuse or grant credit may serve to strengthen the federal character of the procedure by which the recommendations are decided upon and to put political teeth into them. The recommendations may thus become the orientation point for the coordination of national monetary and fiscal policies.

Just one more comment on the structural norms. They are, of course, completely one-sided. They may enforce deflation, or rather disinflation, but they cannot force a reflation of underemployed economies. I do not consider this a serious shortcoming, since, as I have said before, the real problem under modern conditions appears to be one-sided. In fact, it is the most natural problem, if you look at it from a general point of view, that individual units in the economy must be constrained from claiming too large a piece of the pie. This is as true for individuals, corporations, interests groups, and local or regional communities as it is for states. The curious phenomenon that in our macroeconomic affairs we have in the past seemed to escape this law, owing to a unique mixture of ignorance and dogmatism, should not blind us to its basic validity in the real world of today.

So far, I have not touched on the third major tool of stabilization policy, namely, incomes policy. This is related to the very serious problem of cost-push inflation in all its many forms. Constraints with respect to incomes policy are extremely hard to put into credit conditions, since the power of governments in this area is very limited at best. In fact, for all the discussion about wages policy in Sweden and in the Netherlands, there is a very legitimate doubt whether we have been able to depress the Phillips curve at all. If one looks at the relationship between levels of unemployment and the rise of wage rates in different countries, one sees that the curve is not significantly lower for those countries that have made a relatively strong effort at an active wages policy.

Now it may well be that as long as wage bargaining in the Community is still on a national level, the wage-push problem may become somewhat less pressing in the Community. Closer interdependence of markets will tend to increase the elasticity of demand for national labor as a function of national wage rates and thus reduce the power of labor unions. The balance of payments constraint, coupled with the strong anti-inflationary credit policies of the EEC Reserve Fund, will limit the power of national government to provide additional purchasing power so as to bail out labor after excessive wage increases.

Of course this will only be temporary. The problem will reappear on the Community level, when wage bargaining becomes Community-wide rather than national, a development the first signs of which are already appearing. But an incomes policy for the Community as a whole would be a subject for an entire book, and I shall leave the question open because it is, for the time being, not yet of immediate significance to the Community.

In conclusion, I want to make two final comments on the question that I started out with: How realistic is the approach I have indicated, and does it really hold a promise for eventual development toward monetary union?

The first part of the question is the most difficult. Will countries accept the limited discipline in the area of monetary and fiscal policy that is inherent in the conditional credit system I have outlined? The approach I have indicated makes the answer relatively easy. Countries are not forced to give up overtly any real economic sovereignty. Coordination is slipped in through the back door of the mutual assistance and escape clause of the Treaty in case of balance of payments difficulties. Countries would have to accept restrictions on their national freedom of action only in case of balance of payments difficulties and only as a price for obtaining the carrot of Community credit. When the excessive U.S. balance of payments deficits have ceased, and after the full customs union has come into effect, the national balance of payments constraint might become a very tight-fitting harness indeed. Even those countries that are least willing to give up national economic sovereignty might be concerned about the effect of this tight harness on their national growth and employment objective. They may eventually be willing to trade in part of their fiscal and monetary autonomy for a relaxation of the balance of payments constraint.

Once the procedure is set on the track, it seems possible to increase its scope and gradually dissociate the monetary and fiscal discipline from balance of payments difficulties. As I have pointed out before, this will be necessary before any radical steps can be taken toward freedom of capital movements between the member states.

Although such a development is not impossible, it does demand political willingness to submit national policies eventually to Community supervision. For even the stage door carries a clear sign of the play that will be performed: the gradual abdication of the nation in favor of the Community in both the orientation and the instrumentation of general economic policy.

The end of the road will be full monetary union. Once rules, procedures, and institutions for common monetary and fiscal policy exist, the final step toward a common currency is technically a simple one. The national central banks could be transformed into member banks of a Federal Reserve System, with the present Committee of Governors acting as the policy-making board, thus restoring the desirable de facto separation of powers between monetary and fiscal authorities.

But this is very far off, and any speculation about a common European currency is really a speculation about the federation of policy making in the macroeconomic area, a problem that so far has hardly been touched. The European Economic Community still has a very long way to go before it can justify its claim to be more than a simple old-fashioned customs union. For, outside a few really minor areas, that is precisely what it is now and what it will continue to be as long as national governments remain the sole guardians of national macroeconomic policy.

II

COMMON POLICIES IN THE GAULLIST ERA

Almost exactly ten years ago the six member countries of the European Economic Community ended their long and eventful period of courtship by signing the Treaty of Rome. Within ten months after that date, on January 1, 1958, the Common Market was born.

The genetics are rather complex. It is said that the little nine-year-old shows all the traits of his multiple parents—the honesty of the Italian, the sense of humor of the German, the consistency of the Belgian, the emotionality of the Dutch, and the altruism of the French. There are some who even detect a touch of the British inferiority complex, but they are gossips who have been severely reprimanded in public by the self-appointed father of the six fatherlands.

There had been children before, but they did not fare well. Most were stillborn. There is only one surviving—barely surviving—child of the trial marriage or, if you wish, the limited engagement of the Six: the Coal and Steel Community. There is also a twin sister, Euratom. But both of these other children are rather retarded and sickly. They are more and more dependent on their parents and are already dominated by their one lively sister. For the European Economic Community has shown far greater vitality and far greater promise than either of the two other communities, the Coal and Steel Community and Euratom. So far, she has survived the many strains of a *mariage à six* and of the transplantation from the hospitable climate in which she was born, in Rome, to the colder and more rational surroundings in Brussels where she has settled down in the most inappropriately named street one could think of—the Rue de la Joyeuse Entrée, which, literally translated into English, would be something like the "road of joyous entry." Street names in Brussels are bilingual, but fortunately the second language is not English. For the British equivalent of the rue de la Joyeuse Entrée would probably be something like the "avenue of the slammed door."

21

I shall belabor these parables no further because my experience shows that such similes often tend to get out of hand. Instead, I should like to review very briefly the internal accomplishments of the Community to date and then turn to the problems of the present and the future.

The present situation in the European Economic Community is that all impediments to trade among the six countries, as well as the corresponding restrictions on payments, have been practically abolished and will be entirely eliminated on July 1, 1968, a year and a half before the earliest date foreseen in the Treaty of Rome. The differences between the common external tariff of the Community and the national tariffs on products from outside the Community have already been bridged two-thirds of the way and will be eliminated on the same date, which will mark the completion of the customs union of the Six. A common agricultural policy, one of the very thorniest problems that has faced the Six, has been agreed upon and is in the process of being put into effect. With the completion of the agricultural policy, all quotas will soon have disappeared in intra-Community trade. The main lines of competition policy have been worked out and have been codified into Community law. The execution of competition policy has recently made important strides forward as a result of various decisions of the European Court, in particular the Grundig-Consten case, which in one stroke wiped out in interstate commerce among the Six all restrictive practices based on exclusive franchise or on the abuse of patent protection.

The first step in abolishing the fiscal frontiers between the Six was taken by the recent decision to standardize all national systems of turnover taxes in a unified system of taxes on value added. The next step will be to harmonize the tax rates themselves. Discriminatory treatment with regard to the establishment of out-of-state firms has been abolished in a great many areas, and substantial and interesting efforts are being made to harmonize company law in the six countries so as to implement the freedom of establishment and to prevent it from inducing a rush to incorporate in the country that has the least exacting legal requirements. Little progress so far has been made in establishing a unified capital market, as I have shown in the preceding chapter. The legal and economic obstacles to free movement of labor have been substantially reduced by gradually increasing the scope of equal rights without regard to nationality, both in employment and in social security.

Finally, the approach towards a common transport policy is still lagging behind, but it seems probable that substantive decisions will be taken in this area in the near future.

All these steps towards a truly integrated economic system of the Six, modest in some areas and quite advanced in others, have served to increase dramatically the trade among member countries, which by 1965 had more than tripled as compared to the level in 1958, whereas total world trade had advanced by only 70 per cent. It is, of course, true that all these efforts toward economic integration among the Six tend to give a competitive advantage to insiders which is not granted to outsiders. But it is often forgotten that the Common Market has also greatly facilitated the export drive by outsiders, who no longer have to divide their efforts over six markets with often widely divergent conditions of entry. Quite apart from the fact, obvious surely in this country, that some discrimination in favor of interstate as against international trade is inherent in any community, the actual figures belie, and I hope will continue to belie, those who cry protectionism even though the share of outside imports into the Community, calculated as a percentage of the Community's total GNP, has increased rather than decreased.

So much, then, for the achievement of the Community to date. What are the major lessons we have learned in the eight years since the first tariff cut went into effect? The first lesson is common to the European Economic Community and the other efforts in the field of regional free trade, such as Benelux and the European Free Trade Association. In expanding developed economies the establishment of free trade in industrial products meets with very few problems, far fewer certainly than was ever expected. The Treaty of Rome has an elaborate escape clause which allows countries to apply for authorization to take protective measures if any sector or any region of the economy is seriously injured by increased competition due to the Common Market. In all these eight years, the escape clause has been invoked on behalf of industrial products in only a single case, and that for a period of no more than six months. Apparently, industrial firms operating in an expanding market can and do adjust very rapidly to changes in the structure of the market, such as the establishment of a free trade area. This is understandable since they continuously have to make such adjustments in any case under the pressure of technological progress, new products, and new methods, which in many sectors make existing equipment totally obsolete within a few years. Whatever new elements of change free trade may add to this are submerged in the general climate of continuous adjustment and self-propelled renewal and development. French industry, in particular, has found somewhat to its own surprise that it could stand up to German competition and has even built up an enviable export position on the German home market.

Far more difficult are the problems of what I shall call *positive* coordination of economic policy as distinct from the negative coordination that consists in abolishing measures which protect or discriminate on the basis of nationality. I use the term positive coordination in the most general sense, including the harmonization of national laws and regulations as well as the coordination of policy itself. In this area the problems have often turned out to be far more difficult than was expected, and progress, in many cases, has in fact been extremely slow. Already some deadlines contained in the Treaty of Rome have not been met, and it seems likely that in quite a few sectors coordination will not have been achieved before the general deadline of January 1, 1970, the official end of the transitional period of the Treaty.

I need not spell out in detail the difficulties involved in positive coordination of economic policy, since the trials and tribulations of the Community's agricultural policy have been well advertised. And that is one of the very few successful efforts, in the sense that a common solution has been found, whatever one might think of its contents. A very great deal remains to be done. The body of law and the active policies of the government that directly influence our modern economy have grown to immense proportions, and practically all of these affect interstate commerce, as is surely obvious from the experience in this country. Six nations, starting from an entirely different legal and economic basis, face a gigantic task in coordinating all these laws, regulations, and policies to the extent necessary for a proper functioning of the Common Market—a concept which I shall come back to shortly.

The main tasks then that remain are all in the area of positive coordination. Unfortunately, heavy clouds hang over the future of the Community in precisely this area. For one of the partners has announced as its firm policy that it will not proceed to a further federalization of the decision-making process in the Community. In the six months before January 1, 1967, when the Community entered the third and last stage of the transitional period, the

French government refused to cooperate in Community affairs, ostensibly to force progress in agricultural policy but in reality to block the automatic passage towards decision making by majority on a number of major issues, as foreseen in the Treaty of Rome from the third stage on. The conflict was resolved on the surface without major concessions to France, but in reality the federal elements in the Community system of decision making have been virtually suspended.

The limited space at my disposal does not permit me to go into this important question in detail. I may just mention that the position of the true federal, or prefederal, institution of the Community, the European Commission, has been badly and perhaps fatally weakened by restrictions on its freedom of political activity which, though seemingly unimportant, may have served, however, to undercut the European Commission's only really independent source of power vis-à-vis the national governments, namely, a direct appeal to public opinion and private interest groups. Moreover, the unilateral declaration on the part of the French government that it would not abide by majority decisions in its disfavor if France considered its vital national interests threatened may have no legal basis in the Treaty and may have no immediate operational significance, since no such decisions are likely to be taken in any case; but it does nonetheless tend to block further progress towards federalization of the decision-making process in the Community.

How disruptive is this roadblock or, to put it in other terms, how essential to further progress of the Community in the area of positive coordination is a decision-making procedure other than by unanimity? Past experience in this respect is not very encouraging. When neither external threats nor the promise of immediate rewards can pull different nations together, common action invariably becomes slow, difficult, and usually stagnant. A multitude of European organizations bear very silent testimony to this general adage.

This is why the founding fathers of the European Community have built the slow and gradual, but legally inescapable, federalization of decision making into the Treaty of Rome by bringing successively more areas of decision under the rule of majority voting, according to a fixed timetable associated with the three transitional stages of the Community. One might say that the philosophy of the Treaty is to launch the Community by means of a two-stage rocket. The first rocket was to lift the ship off the pad and set it on a straight upward course by establishing free trade among the Six according to a fixed and irreversible timetable— irreversible, that is, after the point of no return had been passed by the formal and unanimous vote of January, 1962, which marked the passage to the second stage of the Community. The momentum of free trade was supposed to carry the Community through the many difficulties of the first eight years of its existence and did in fact do so. The irrevocable commitment of the member states and the irreversible course mapped out in advance induced business to adjust itself to the new environment, in fact to anticipate the later stages by planning investment as a function of the future course of the Community. Free trade created an important momentum that pushed the initial venture through the stage of decision making by unanimity. Granted, most decisions were package deals, but they would never have been devised or accepted had not the deadlines of the Treaty and the pressure of economic interests pushed governments into positive action. This was the first manifestation of the *solidarité de fait,* the community of interest based on economic reality, which has always played such a large role in the thinking of those concerned with European integration.

The second stage of the rocket was to fire automatically on January 1, 1966, when the first rocket was practically burned out with the virtual achievement of the customs union. The second rocket would, as was originally thought, provide new thrust, thanks to the institutional and political fuel provided by the introduction of policy making by majority vote rather than by unanimity. This would greatly strengthen the position of the pre-federal institution, the European Community, and give it the power to forge ahead in the many areas of common policy which were to turn the customs union into a true economic community with completely free movement of goods, services, and factors of production, undistorted by differences in public policy and unhindered by the great many nontariff barriers that still make export from one Community country to another a more difficult, costly, and risky affair than selling on the home market.

Lifted into orbit in these two stages, the rocket would then proceed on its own, fueled by the mutually reinforcing pressures of increasing economic interpenetration and of common policies decided upon by majority vote. These are the fundamental economic and political dynamics of the Treaty as conceived in the exciting years before 1958. But can we still go ahead, and where are we going now that the intervention of France has prevented the firing of the second rocket? How much thrust is left in the first rocket, assuming that the second will continue to malfunction?

Again, past experience is not encouraging. Benelux developed successfully into a full customs union ten or fifteen years ago, but since then progress has been at a snail's pace. To be sure, a great deal has been achieved in the unification of laws and regulations that affect commerce among the three countries and in the harmonization of tax structures. But the coordination of major economic policies has stagnated. The coordination of monetary policy, of policies aimed at stabilization and balanced economic growth, with the final objective of full monetary union—all these areas have been extensively discussed, but no real progress has been made. The pressures of private interests and political forces pushing towards further integration in these areas apparently are not very strong. As one moves from the establishment of free trade and nondiscrimination, via the harmonization of specific laws and policies, towards the final area of coordination in matters of general macroeconomic policy, the interests involved become very indirect and very diffused. At the same time, as one moves along this series of steps, one gets closer and closer to the very heart of national economic sovereignty: full employment policies, fiscal structure, the management of money, the industrial and regional structure of the economy, and so forth. The political pressures making for integration decrease, the resistance to it increases, and progress becomes increasingly difficult.

All this leads to the essential question I would like to discuss: To what extent is the harmonization of laws and the coordination of economic policies in these various areas essential to achieving the basic economic purposes of European integration? Or, to turn the question around, what would be the result if the community's further development were to stagnate and it stopped at the point where a customs union has been achieved but before economic policy is fully and effectively coordinated?

Let me say to begin with that I want to make no prediction as to the likelihood of this development, since it depends on a great many factors which neither I nor, perhaps, anyone outside the Elysée could evaluate with any degree of confidence. But I believe it is fair to say that such a state of stagnation is not very unlikely,

given the political situation in France and the growing sense of frus-
tration in Brussels. It is, in any event, worth discussion as a warn-
ing to us all, for the impact of such a development on world affairs
would be momentous, if not disastrous. If Western Europe were to
drift into a situation where one or two preferential arrangements
severely limited the national freedom to carry out an active economic policy without replacing it by effective policy-making machinery on the Community level, the largest trading area in the
world would be immobilized, unable to discharge the responsibilities which its economic potential has laid upon it. The situation
might then well be worse than it would have been without the integration movement.

This brings me to one final point before I pass to the discussion
of economic policy itself and the coordination of policy in the
Community. It concerns the entry of Britain and other EFTA
countries into the Community. The smaller countries, including
Italy, always did and do now welcome British entry, not only for
political reasons but also to provide a new dynamic element in the
Community, just as Britain is seeking admission to stimulate her
own economy. But does this development, if it materializes, really
change, in the long run, the basic political and economic parameters of the problem?

Ever since the first moves toward economic integration among
the Six, the smaller countries and, in particular, the Netherlands,
have found themselves in an agonizing dilemma, having to choose
between two alternative methods of attaining their ultimate political and economic objectives. This ultimate goal of their integra-
tionist policies has never been seriously in dispute: the federation
of all Western Europe into a community of law with a truly federal
structure, tied to North America in a strong Atlantic Alliance, and
economically open to the outside. But the methods of achieving
this goal have been and still are the subject of sometimes quite
heated controversy. The political situation in Western Europe in
the 1950's polarized the more immediate policy objectives into
two mutually exclusive alternative roads, the proponents of which
have been labeled "maximalists" and "minimalists" respectively.
The maximalists have consistently favored a strengthening of the
existing communities and have refused to compromise on the
road to federation by admitting members that would not be willing to subscribe to the federal aspects of the Treaty. They main-
tained that this was the only realistic road away from the sterile

intergovernmental arrangements that have proliferated in Western Europe and elsewhere. If it had the initial effect of estranging the Community from the rest of Europe, which in the 1950's was not ready to accept the federal idea, this was the price that had to be paid. But it is, or it was, according to this view, the only way to form a strong enough nucleus to attract others into the federal fold. The United Kingdom's request for admission to the Community on the basis of the Rome Treaty appeared to bear out the maximalists' point of view.

The minimalists, on the other hand, reverse these priorities, stressing the importance of first extending the Community outward and then building up strong common policies and institutions, for they fear that the maximalists' approach will tend to harden the nucleus into an exclusive club, admission into which would become more difficult as time went on. For, they argued, the admission of new members would require greater adjustments on the part of members and nonmembers alike as the Community progressed. Economic and political inbreeding would tend to reinforce this process. Although this view is not directly vindicated by France's veto of British entry into the Community, a decision that was clearly based on other motives, the centripetal forces built up in the Community, in the form of powerful established interests committed to its survival, did show up in the lack of a strong response on the part of the other five countries.

The policy of the smaller countries, and of the Dutch in particular, has always vacillated between these two approaches, the minimal and the maximal, and it has often seemed internally inconsistent, a fact which the sixth member has been all too ready to point out. It does seem a hardly coherent policy to insist on strong supranational procedures and institutions within the Community, and then to drop these ideals without a tear as a price for the admission of outsiders. It is the sheer cussedness of history that at the very time when the best of both worlds appeared attainable, when the United Kingdom expressed its willingness to accept the constitutional procedures and the institutions of the Common Market, France not only vetoed British admission but shortly afterwards also proceeded to sabotage the federal provisions of the Treaty and to undermine the position of the federal institution.

Now that Britain is once more seeking entry into the Community, the question may well be asked whether, notwithstanding

British willingness to accept the federal provisions of the Treaty, the Community is not essentially taking a turn toward the minimalists' approach. For the federal character of the decision-making process has already been badly weakened, and the entry of Britain, as well as of most or all of the other EFTA countries, is unlikely to bring any change in this respect. In fact, a further weakening of the European Commission and a strengthening of the national veto may well be France's price if she is to agree at all. This would leave the Community with only one device for common decision-making: the package deal. It is true that the Community has used the technique of the package deal with some considerable success in the past, when it had to deal with only six members and when it was operating under the pressure of the irreversible moves toward free trade. But this same technique may well become completely unwieldy when the number of national accounts to be balanced in the deal increases from the present six to something like ten or eleven. Moreover, the package deal may be less appropriate for initiating and carrying out common policies that are not directly related to free trade and therefore are not pushed along by the fixed timetable of automatic tariff reductions.

This brings me once more to the original question which I can now no longer escape: the economic significance of the various areas of common policy and the consequences of a failure to co-ordinate national efforts effectively in these areas.

In discussing the significance of common policy I would like to focus on the concept of the European firm. For I strongly believe that the real payoff of economic integration is the emergence of corporate units which are scaled to the dimensions of the total market and operate with complete disregard of national boundaries. The European firm as so conceived would sell anywhere in the entire market, obtain its material inputs from the most favorable source, obtain funds wherever available at the lowest rates, and draw its labor and management from anywhere within the Community—all this without regard to any risk involved in getting too dependent on out-of-state sources of supply or on out-of-state markets for its products. Such firms would have fully integrated operations in the entire market, subcontracting, merging, and dispersing their plants to take full advantage of optimum conditions of location, and they would hold their assets denominated in any Community currency without preference or distinction.

Only such firms attain the size that is required to be able to complete in modern conditions, not only in terms of short-run efficiency but also (and in the opinion of many, primarily) in terms of research and development, the ultimate engines of economic progress as well as the major sources of profits in an age of rapid technological change. It is not just coincidence that American firms on the whole spend far more on research and development than their European counterparts and that at the same time they also tend to be larger. There is a vital scale factor here, borne out by direct evidence of the relation between size and the proportion of corporate income spent on research and development. In the Netherlands, for example, practically all industrial research is carried out by the five largest companies, a degree of activity completely out of proportion to their contribution to the national product. If it is true that a technology gap exists in Europe (and I have no doubt that it does if one compares the whole of European industry with the whole of American industry, allowing for the difference in GNP) then it is due to the scale of corporate operations. Moreover, without the European firm and the diffusion of regional economic interests which it creates, large-scale public development programs, and their vital technological fallout, are hamstrung by the need to divide operations so as to produce a positive balance sheet for each participating state. The experience in Euratom is a clear sign.

Of course the markets of most European countries are large enough to support firms of a size comparable to their U.S. counterparts. And several of the smaller countries in particular have built up large firms on the basis of exports. But the separate European markets are *not* large enough to support several such large firms in a directly competitive setting. Moreover, the sectioning of the market into relatively small national units deprives the industry of the potentially very important external economies that derive from standardization in the factor markets, when they buy and subcontract on a common market rather than on a set of separate submarkets that are insufficiently communicating. The deluge of present problems and the efforts towards standardization of weights and measures in the European Economic Community bear eloquent witness to the importance of this factor.

Free trade and the elimination of overt discrimination on the basis of nationality are not enough to establish the conditions for the emergence of European firms, in this sense, on a sufficiently broad scale. Both in Benelux and in the EEC, trade has very significantly increased upon the removal of tariff barriers. A large proportion of Frenchmen now drive German and Italian cars, where one used to see very few cars of other than French make that bore French license plates. Conversely, great numbers of Italians and Germans now drive French-made cars. The automobile firms have encroached on each others' markets to a significant extent, and the trade in automobiles has expanded dramatically. But the short-term "welfare effects" of this sort of exchange turn out to be pretty small. In fact, notwithstanding the considerable scientific efforts spent on trying to determine the welfare effect of the EEC, the results always turn out to be disappointingly small, somewhere on the order of ½ to 1 per cent of present GNP for the entire period between 1958 and 1965, which is surely no great achievement when projected against the background of a total real growth of GNP during the same period of about 45 per cent, and considering the immense efforts that have gone into establishing free trade and the great expectations it engendered. To be sure, the dynamic effects of the EEC may have been more substantial than the static welfare effects, but what evidence there is is neither wholly convincing nor very impressive. Nor have the long-term effects in promoting larger production units so far been noticeable. The Common Market has induced quite a few mergers, but they have been mostly on the national level, and those that have involved firms in different countries have not, in most cases, led to a complete integration of operations. The individual firms have usually retained their operational identity and have pooled their efforts only in selected areas.

Is this just traditionalism, conventional patterns of doing business that are hard to change? It might seem so, considering that the subsidiaries of American firms that have started operations in the Common Market since 1958 have been far more ready than European firms to adjust their operations to the scale of the total EEC market. However, I believe there is more behind this than just traditionalism. That is undoubtedly part of the explanation, but not the whole, if only because American firms operating in Europe have sometimes shown a similar tendency to split up along national lines.

Another part of the explanation, and perhaps the most important part, is the continued existence of many nontariff barriers to trade. As long as these are still significant it may not pay for established firms to integrate their operations too closely. This is different for the new firm, which plans its operations as a function of the anticipated future structure of the market. If the new firm is at the same time financially strong enough to set up operations on a European scale, the conditions for the emergence of the European firm are satisfied. Paradoxically, this is true in particular for the subsidiaries of the giant U.S. concerns, which in a very real sense are the first true European firms to emerge. But that, of course, is not enough, since the investment of these firms is only a small percentage of the total European industrial investments. The real impetus must come from mergers of European firms across state borders. Before such movement can gather force a great deal will have to be done in eliminating the countless invisible barriers to trade which still make interstate trade in the Common Market in many areas more difficult, more time consuming, and hence more costly than national sales, thus tending to preserve the national bias in the structure of production and sales. Differences in regulations in the areas of public health, safety, labeling and packaging, and weights and measures, together with differences in company law, in fiscal structure, in conditions of establishment, and in innumerable other forms of public regulation of production and commerce, tend to act as effective barriers to fully integrated interstate operations, even if no direct national discrimination is involved.

A perfect example of this is the difference in the admissible weight of trucks on the roads of various countries. In some countries the maximum is 13 tons per axle; in others it is only 10, as a result of past decisions to construct roads for one weight limit rather than the other. This difference, which involves no overt discrimination at all, nevertheless effectively hampers the free and undistorted competition among truckers of different national origins. It is, in a sense, a purely technical problem, but one that involves public expenditure, and hence a political decision.

Harmonization of laws and regulations in this as well as in all of the other areas I have mentioned is required in order effectively to reduce the invisible barriers to the level where the European firm can live with them, as the U.S. firm can live with some limited differences in the internal legal and economic framework of the different states in the United States. But such harmonization implies that future changes in the laws and regulations concerned can be made only by common accord. Otherwise, the achievements could at any time be destroyed by national action, possibly for national reasons that are quite legitimate but nonetheless destructive of the Common Market. It requires, in other words, common policies, a common process of decision making, in all the areas concerned, since no laws and regulations are ever made for eternity. Many, in fact, are instruments of short-term social and economic policy, such as tax rates, subsidies, conditions of entry, regulation of establishment, etc., which are all manipulated frequently in the interests of stabilization, regional development, social policy, balanced economic growth, and other national objectives.

Moreover, many of these invisible barriers can be removed only after various factors that distort competitive conditions have been eliminated. Again, this requires extensive harmonization of existing measures in such areas as taxation, company law, and conditions of establishment. And again, this leads to the need for common policies in all those areas that utilize these measures as instruments of public policy.

It is my conviction that ultimately the most essential area of coordination by far is that of general economic policy, typified by its major objectives of stabilization and balanced economic growth. I base this proposition on two major arguments.

First, the absence of effective coordination in the area of general economic policy poses a vital threat to the survival of the Common Market. As long as these policies are still a purely national responsibility, the national state may at times be severely tempted or actually forced by the pre-eminence of its national objectives and by internal political pressures to employ measures which upset free movement within the Common Market, either directly by reimposing restrictions or indirectly by the use of policy tools such as tax rates, which had been harmonized before. The national state may, for example, raise taxes in order to combat inflation. It may reintroduce restrictions on trade and the free movement of labor to fight unemployment at home or reimpose certain restrictions on international payments or on capital movements in order to safeguard the balance of payments. Benelux offers quite a few examples of unilateral raising of tax rates as part of a national stabilization program, after the rates had been laboriously harmonized in a long and arduous process of negotiation. It is obvious that such measures badly hamper any real progress towards harmonization and therefore towards the real integration of the markets, which is a precondition for the emergence of the European firm. They may even lead to a progressive disintegration of the

Common Market if unilateral measures of one state lead other states to take similar steps. The same is true in the area of structural economic policy. In the absence of an effective coordination of their regional and structural policies as a whole, the states may easily revert to national measures, as is all too clearly shown by the disintegration of the European Coal and Steel Community and Euratom.

My first argument can be summarized in the proposition that effective coordination in the area of general economic policy, both short and long term, is essential to prevent the states from going back on their obligations in the Common Market, for the simple reason that these general objectives are of such overriding national importance that they dwarf the interests of integration in any particular field.

My second argument is closely related to the first, but it is still a separate issue. Even if the states do not actually take any unilateral measures, the fact that they *might* do so is an effective barrier against firms' organizing their operations with complete disregard of national boundaries. This is most dramatically illustrated in the area of money. Comparisons are always somewhat misleading, and the present one is overemployed as well, but it may help to visualize the vital importance of monetary union if one imagines each state of the American union to have its own currency and to have the authority to change the parity and impose exchange restrictions. Can one imagine a corporation like General Motors being organized in the same manner under those conditions as it is now? The currencies of the separate states might well be stable and fully convertible in most cases and for most of the time, but is it likely that all states, if independent in this respect, would always resist the temptation to overextend themselves for possibly very valid reasons, regarded from the state point of view? Might not an ambitious growth objective induce a state to resort to direct restrictions or to exchange variation in order to correct the deficit on its balance of payments resulting from excess home investment? It is all too obvious what this event, or even the risk of such events, would do to the structure of American business. Likewise, continued monetary autonomy of the European states is surely not a climate likely to foster the growth of the European firm.

I conclude that common policies, especially in the areas of general economic policy, are essential for the survival of the Community and for the realization of its real economic payoff. Elsewhere in this volume I present some ideas on what is involved here and how the objectives could be achieved.

But behind it all is the one vital point on which I would like to end the present discussion. Viable common policies require a federal structure of decision making. The resurgence of European nationalism after the initial enthusiasm for the federal idea obstructs progress in this direction. The next few years may well decide whether Western Europe will slide back into the relative decline which, without integration, had become inevitable when the separate European state ceased to be the relevant scale in economic affairs, as it so obviously is in matters of defense; or whether the internal dynamics of the EEC and the force of reason will create sufficient economic and political momentum to break through the barrier of national sovereignty and enable Europe to resume its share of responsibility in world affairs which its history, its economic potential, its large share in international trade, and its many ties with this country so clearly impose on it.

III

PLANNING FOR GROWTH

Introduction

I hesitated for some time before settling on a title for the last chapter of this study. Although I admit that the desire to be just a little provocative played its part in my finally choosing "Planning for Growth," there is a real problem of communication here. The European Community has adopted "medium-term economic policy" to describe my topic. Apart from being rather dull, this formula conveys very little beyond the fact that we are dealing with economic policies that cover a period of about four to five years, conventionally denoted as "medium term." But this is not the essence of what the Community, and the individual countries as well, are trying to accomplish under the heading of medium-term economic policy. Most public endeavors—in such areas as, for example, agriculture, transport, energy, and regional development— are carried out on the basis of policy plans that cover at least a medium-term period. Is medium-term economic policy simply a label to denote all those separate efforts that have more than a purely short-run perspective?

In choosing the title "Planning for Growth" I have attempted to indicate that something more is involved; that the essence of what we are dealing with is not a set of specific policies but the orientation of specific policies towards economic growth. It is really not a separate policy area at all, but a comprehensive policy *framework* which brings together all the separate public endeavors which directly or indirectly affect economic growth. It is thus concerned not only with measures that are aimed specifically at stimulating economic growth—such as fiscal and other incentives for investment, support for research and development, improvement of occupational and regional mobility, and the like—but also with all the other areas of policy which, although affecting economic growth, have as their primary objectives such other (often social) goals as the protection of agricultural incomes, the support of coal mining, or the development of depressed areas. Medium-term economic policy adds a growth dimension to these separate goals. In other words, its main purpose is to bring together all these separate public endeavors in the framework of a coherent (i.e., an integrated and internally consistent) policy plan which takes account of the interrelationships among the separate areas, in particular their impact on economic growth.

This formula is probably sufficiently obscure to convince you that this whole policy area is still very much in a state of flux conceptually and politically, as well as in practice. The actual situations in the various countries of the European Economic Community differ considerably from one another. Some have a very elaborate planning framework, France in particular, whereas other countries, with Germany as the principal example, have a very loose form of policy coordination. To make matters worse, this whole area is also highly seasoned with emotional and dogmatic connotations, evoked whenever the concept of "planning" is applied to the economy as a whole. Planning is idolized by some, in terms well exemplified by the late Oskar Lange, who once compared the economic systems of East and West to a modern jet and an antiquated Zeppelin, respectively. The eastern airplane would, in his metaphor, be guided purposefully on its course by highly sophisticated instruments and trained pilots who know exactly where they are going and who consciously choose the best way of getting there. The Western economies, on the other hand, would just be drifting along on the economic currents, without rudder and without purposeful direction.

This type of characterization, as well as the counterpart tendency to worship the competitive market system and reject any active planning is, fortunately, passé. We all realize that both economic systems are mixed, and many of us see abundant evidence for Tinbergen's theory that the decentralized collectivism of the East and the guided capitalism of the West show marked tendencies to converge. National planning as such is no longer controversial in the Western economies, as witnessed by the universal acceptance of stabilization policy. To be sure, it is not fashionable to use the term planning in this context. But if we look at it objectively, stabilization policy exhibits all the essential characteristics of national planning: the targets are set by collective decision, the policies are worked out in the framework of a short-term projection which encompasses the entire economy, and the actual measures taken intervene quite extensively in the private sector.

In principle, "planning for growth" need not be more controversial than stabilization policy. Most countries have, implicitly or explicitly, accepted certain growth targets. The twenty-one states of the Organization for Economic Cooperation and Development (encompassing Western Europe, North America, and, since 1964, Japan) have, for example, set themselves a collective target of 50 per cent growth of their combined GNP during the decade of the 1960's. The major specific instruments of growth policy, which aim at stimulating mobility in the economy as well as investment in human, technological, and material capital, are utilized by all. Moreover, all governments for one reason or another intervene quite actively in some sectors of the economy; adding a growth dimension to these policies does not seem particularly difficult to accept. Growth policy does, however, tend to become controversial when it involves detailed selective intervention in the private sector of the economy, aimed at correcting or preventing structural imbalances that threaten to impede the growth of the economy as a whole. This might take the form of stimulating some sectors and holding back others by means of such devices as selective fiscal incentives or disincentives, selective credit facilities, and special subsidies. The more selective these measures, the more specific are the implied targets for private enterprise; and private decision making, with its complements of private responsibility and risk taking tends increasingly to abdicate in favor of decisions by the public authorities. The extent to which such a transfer of decision making is desirable or undesirable is one of the major areas of conflict between left and right in economic policy. The issue is very much alive on the national scene of the individual Common Market countries, and it is reflected in the efforts of the Community.

The prevailing opinion and the actual practice differ substantially from one country of the Community to another. An understanding of the major factors involved is essential in order to bring out the background of the forces that are at work in shaping Community policy in this area. That is why I propose to spend a relatively large part of this chapter on *national* planning for growth. If I seem to wander far from our main concern, the European Economic Community, it is because the Community's economic policy is in many respects, and certainly in this one, still very much a derivative of national policies. Before going into the subject of planning for growth, let me say that it is exceedingly difficult in

practice to draw a sharp line between the controversial and the un-
controversial in growth policy—between those cases in which it constitutes no more than an additional dimension to measures that are
primarily aimed at other objectives (such as support for agriculture) and those cases in which the growth objective is itself the
main drive behind detailed and selective intervention in the private sector. Often the chain of causality and motive is hard to establish. Countries may practice detailed intervention primarily for
reasons other than stimulating overall economic growth and may
be led to comprehensive planning for growth as a means of giving
due weight to the growth objective in relation to these other goals
of public policy. On the other hand, countries that engage in comprehensive planning for growth may be led to utilize detailed and
selective measures in order to achieve their growth objectives. In
attempting to understand the real significance of planning for
growth in the individual countries of Western Europe and in the
EEC, we must keep these two different perspectives in mind, even
though in actual situations it may be difficult or even impossible
to determine which side of the looking-glass represents reality and
which political fiction.

The National Framework

Projecting medium-term economic developments

It is obviously as essential for an effective growth policy as it is
for short-term stabilization to have an adequate technique of forecasting economic developments. Already on this level there are
wide differences among the actual practices in the different countries of the Community. Germany, on one end of the scale, relies
on forecasting techniques that are similar to those employed for
short-term projections. Projections are arrived at by econometric
as well as eclectic methods; these methods may involve quite in-
tensive research into private investment plans, but they do not require an active participation on the part of the business world. The
other countries of the Community, however, following the example of France, have built up elaborate institutional machineries
which assign a very active role to representatives of business in ar-
riving at medium-term economic projections. One might look
at these techniques as providing an institutionalized planning

framework both for the public authorities and for the private sector.

Although the question of forecasting techniques is not immediately relevant to the policies of the EEC, since projections for the Community as a whole are still arrived at essentially by adding the national forecasts of the individual member countries, it may nevertheless be worth while to spend a few minutes on a review of the institutionalized forecasting techniques practiced in France and other countries. They constitute an important element in the efforts at planning for growth of all countries except Germany, and they may also exercise a significant influence on the orientation of these countries' growth policies. In discussing this question, I shall take my examples mostly from France and the Netherlands, because among those countries that engage in this type of institutionalized forecasting (which excludes Germany), France and the Netherlands are more or less at opposite ends of the scale with respect to the direct influence of the projection, or "plan," on public policy. The public authorities in France make fairly extensive use of selective policy instruments to influence private decisions when the projected structure of private investment does not correspond with the government's short- and medium-term objectives of balanced economic growth and social equity, whereas in the Netherlands direct public intervention is in principle limited to general growth policies such as those mentioned earlier (general tax incentives for investment, etc.). We shall have to examine more closely in the course of this discussion the distinction between these two approaches to see whether it is as sharp and clear as it might appear to be at first sight.

In all countries that engage in this type of exercise, the essence of the "planning framework" is to simulate the results of economic development for the coming four or five years. It is really an elaborate management decision game which in principle encompasses the entire economy.

The game is played by representatives of business (in most countries including labor as well as management), organized in a number of so-called "vertical committees" that cover each of the major sectors into which the economy is divided for the purpose of the game. In France, for example, twenty-two such vertical working parties participated in the preparation of the Fourth Plan (covering the period 1962-65), for sectors such as agriculture, transport, power, steel, construction, and so on. In addition, most countries also have various "horizontal" committees that deal with problems common to many or all sectors of the economy, such as research and development, manpower, education, regional development, and the like.

The government enters the game in two roles. It acts more or less like a common player in those areas where it has assumed direct management responsibilities, ranging from the public sector itself (public works, nationalized industry, public utilities, etc.) to such sectors as agriculture and energy, where its policies are an important factor in business decisions. The government also enters the game in a typically public role, by indicating any changes in the rules which it intends to make during the coming period: changes in tax rates, commercial policies, and so on.

The game is usually administered by a more or less independent agency, the "Commissariat Général du Plan" in France and the "Central Planning Bureau" in the Netherlands. Incidentally, the name of the Dutch Central Planning Bureau is typical of the semantic confusion that abounds in this whole area, for the Bureau's "planning" consists solely in making economic projections. It has no target-setting or executive responsibilities whatever. However, since most countries seem to use the word planning in describing their forecasting agencies, I shall continue to refer to the administrator of the management decision game as the planning bureau.

Now that we know the players and the umpire, let us see how the game is played. I must apologize in advance for probably failing to convey the true spirit of the game. As with any game, one can really understand its point only by participating for a while or watching it very closely for a considerable time. I am in a good position to appreciate the difficulties involved, since I still do not understand the fine points of your national sports, even though I have watched a few games of baseball and American football.

As a rule, the medium-term planning game is initiated by the planning bureau, which sets up a rough blueprint of economic development in the next five years on the basis of a more or less sophisticated model and of estimates and assumptions concerning the parameters of the model. The most interesting feature of this first draft is its assumptions concerning public policy, as these will already reflect differences between countries in the policy content of medium-term planning. One might conceivably envisage a "neutral" projection by assuming that government policy remains unchanged. But just what does that mean? To pick one area, does it mean a constant level of government expenditure, a constant rate of increase equal to that of national income, or any of the endless other interpretations of unchanged policy that one could think up? Basically, what is done in practice is to focus on the macro-economic growth rate as the key assumption—or, if you wish, the key target—of the model. The planning bureau will try a few alter-native macroeconomic growth rates and run these through the model in order to see what their implications are for other major variables such as the balance of payments, employment, price stability, etc., under various assumptions concerning public policy. It might then select a particular version either on its own authority or in a dialogue with the government.

In France the growth rate to be adopted has been the result of an explicit public decision, which gives it the flavor of a national policy target. For the decision to accept a certain growth rate and the values of the associated macroeconomic variables (balance of payments, employment, and so on) implies an intention on the part of the public authorities to use the available policy instru-ments to ensure that the targets are met as nearly as possible. In the Netherlands, on the other hand, the choice of the growth rate is the result of a dialogue between the planning bureau and public authorities, the planning bureau being free in principle to follow its own judgment on the basis of whatever information it receives as to the intentions of the government with regard to future policy objectives and instruments. Already at this point it appears that the difference between the two approaches is rather subtle and difficult to define precisely: the choice of a growth rate may be called a "target," as in France or a "projection," incorporating certain ideas about future public policy, as in the Netherlands. But in reality the two could be very similar in everything but appear-ance. And appearances in this whole game are highly deceptive. In the Netherlands the figures on the rate of growth, the balance of payments, and the other major variables, as they appear in the pro-visional blueprint, are really just a reflection of what the public objectives are thought to be and of the tools which the govern-ment is assumed to be willing to employ. If the major objective is stability and the only tools are those of traditional fiscal and monetary policy, the blueprint will still show a definite rate of growth. The numerical value and character of the blueprint in the Dutch case will presumably be different from the French situation, where the growth rate is a specific objective of government policy, to be pursued with a whole host of specific tools. But in both cases *a* rate of growth will pop out of the model, and in both cases it is to *some* extent a target variable, since it is influenced by public policy.

Let us disregard these underlying issues for the moment and go back to our national management decision game. The provisional blueprint, which will usually be disaggregated with respect to the sectors involved in the national decision game, will serve as the kickoff for the game by being submitted for discussion to the various working parties. The representatives of industry will suggest amendments to the forecast for their sector, on the basis of current investment plans and of their specific knowledge of present and future conditions in that sector. There will be some interaction already in this stage between the blueprint and the expectations of business, since the blueprint will contain certain indications on variables that enter into business anticipations, such as the total rate of growth of the economy, the output and demand in competitive and complementary sectors, and the like. The results of these sector discussions, in the form of amendments to the original blueprint, will be reintegrated into the total model by the umpire. In doing this, the planning bureau may well find that a summation of the individual forecasts no longer leads to an internally consistent projection. Often this will show up in the detailed examination of particular aspects of the model in the horizontal committees. It may be found, for example, that the total needs of the economy for a particular type of labor, as implied by the aggregated production plans of the separate sectors, exceeds the supply that is likely to be forthcoming. Such shortages or surpluses imply changes in relative prices which can be run through the model. This will lead to an adjustment of the blueprint to re-establish internal consistency.

The adjusted blueprint will then be fed back to the working parties who have the next move in the game. By a process of successive approximation, the game will finally lead to a consistent projection, reflecting the investment and output plans of business, as modified in the course of the game, as well as the policies which the government intends to pursue in order to attain its objectives. The final projection is referred to as the "plan" in France and simply as the "medium-term projection" in the Netherlands.

This is not the place to go into the advantages and disadvantages of the management decision game in its different national manifestations. As should be obvious from the description, the game is more than just another method of medium-term forecasting employing a special procedure for gathering data about investment plans. By actively engaging business in the exercise, it aims not only at improving the forecast—econometric projections of investment behavior still being very inadequate, certainly on a disaggregated level—but also at providing a direct feedback from forecast to business decision. Participation gives an orientation to decisions that pure information would not provide. This is why countries engaging in this type of exercise are sometimes characterized as *"économies orientées,"* oriented economies.

The game simulates the successive approximation to economic equilibrium by which the market mechanism operates. The price signals of the actual market system are, in a sense, always too late because they register scarcity or overcapacity once it has already developed. If the planning framework serves to anticipate the signals and to induce the necessary adjustments before actual scarcity or overcapacity develops, the economic waste produced by these "errors" may be reduced. This is relatively unimportant as long as the feedback mechanism of the price system operates smoothly and rapidly to eliminate any shortages or surpluses that may appear. But in many sectors of the economy, individual production units have become so large in relation to the size of the market that continuous marginal adjustments of capacity are no longer possible. Under these conditions the feedback mechanism of the price system tends to operate imperfectly, i.e., to produce relatively large errors and long time-lags before they are corrected. Undoubtedly this is one of the major reasons why so many countries in Europe have in recent years established some kind of institutional machinery for carrying out the type of national management decision game I have just described. But even in the economic Arcadia of the small-sized enterprise, dynamic instabilities are not unheard of. By anticipating the outcome of the market, the game purports to rip the cobweb, well known in price theory, before the market gets caught in it.

Of course, any claim that this type of "planning" would always succeed in keeping the economy on a path of rapid and balanced economic growth, uninterrupted by structural adjustments or dynamic instability, would be highly exaggerated. The projections may not be very good, especially in an open economy where an important part of demand must be estimated exogenously.

Technological progress, unanticipated shifts in consumption, and what not may completely upset the predictions. But these deficiencies are in the nature of things future and are no less true for private expectations that do not benefit from any systematic national projection. It is hard to deny that the increased knowledge, however little, and the effective dissemination of that knowledge provided by the exercise constitute valuable—and in practice highly valued—additional tools for management in the private as well as the public sector. One may question whether the results justify the elaborate efforts, and certainly the evidence provided by the experience of France and Germany is not convincing one way or the other; but the cost of planning is not a major point in the European debate. The major potential drawbacks of the planning effort (to be set against its potential advantages) are twofold. First, the planning framework may weaken competition by almost inviting agreements on investment, pricing, and output on the part of the business representatives engaged in the exercise. Whether this inherent threat is a reality and, if so, whether it can or cannot be effectively offset by an active antitrust policy are among the controversial issues in this whole area. Secondly, the planning exercise may lead to more, and particularly more detailed, public intervention in private enterprise. The last point brings us to the subject of medium-term economic *policy,* which I want to discuss briefly before turning to the developments in the European Economic Community.

Medium-term economic policy

The major controversies about planning for growth and also its greatest positive potential arise in the area of medium-term economic policy. Let me first state some of the positive points and then go into the areas of contention. But first one preliminary comment: the essential element of medium-term economic policy as a tool of planning for growth is that every separate policy measure be considered a part of a comprehensive policy plan, which is conceived in the framework of a disaggregated projection of the medium-term development of the economy as a whole. As I have mentioned before, it is not the separate policy measures themselves, but the all-embracing framework that constitutes the essence of planning for growth.

The most obvious advantage of the planning framework to the public authorities is the element of information. If there is some doubt about the use of this type of information to business, there surely is none in the case of the government. The government must fashion its policies as a function of future developments in the economy as a whole. In many cases government action is highly complementary to developments in the private sector. Familiar examples of such direct links are road building, education, and regional development efforts. But the same holds *a fortiori* for government policies in "problem sectors" such as agriculture, transport, and energy: the measures to be taken serve as corrections of the market mechanism and must therefore be based largely on an assessment of what the future situation would be without such intervention.

Another, and in my opinion even more important, aspect of the planning exercise is that it forces the government to coordinate policy within the public sector as a whole. In practice, public policy is usually far from coherent and internally consistent. The measures taken in the various areas for which the public authorities carry a responsibility are often disjointed and sometimes even conflicting rather than mutually supporting. In many instances the various departments of the government, local authorities, and public agencies pursue their own limited tasks with almost complete disregard of other public objectives, even though their particular concerns are often merely different aspects of one and the same problem. Examples of the interrelationships between responsibilities of different branches of government are legion: the development of depressed areas, for example, may be at the same time a problem of agricultural policy, of providing economic infrastructure (transport, education, etc.), of fiscal and other incentives, of efforts by public utilities, of local initiatives, and so on. The national planning framework, in forcing the government to submit a policy plan for the entire public sector, tends to induce more coordination among these separate departments, simply because the government can hardly afford to come up with a plan that is internally inconsistent.

This point has been important on the level of the European Community as well. One of the major difficulties experienced by the European Coal and Steel Community has been that it has only a limited area of responsibility. The problems posed by the structural decline of European coal mining cannot be adequately dealt with in the limited context of the Coal and Steel Community itself. The relevant measures involve not only competing forms of energy that are outside of ECSC's area of competence (oil, natural gas, nuclear energy) but also policies to attract new industries to the coal mining areas, retraining and resettlement of workers, readaptation of the other sectors in the local economy that depend on coal mining, and the like. Most of these measures are outside the ECSC. It is therefore no wonder that the impetus for an integrated structural policy in the Community has come primarily from Luxembourg.

A final positive aspect to be mentioned is that the medium-term planning exercise may serve to make public policy more consistent, not only with respect to different policy areas but also over time. The medium-term framework tends to reduce the emphasis on immediate objectives and increase the relative weight of structural goals in economic policy. Thus, it may favor a shift towards policy that is aimed at real adaptation and adjustment to structural changes in the economy rather than at providing temporary protection, which so often tends to perpetuate itself and hamper long-run adaptation. Moreover, the medium-term perspective may lend support to short-term stabilization of the economy, especially in the vital area of incomes policy, both by making the long-term dangers of overextension explicit and by making it possible as well as realistic to consider long-range benefits (profit-sharing, security of employment, etc.) in return for temporary restraint.

After this eulogy, let us pass on to the controversial aspects of medium-term policy in a planning framework.

As I have already mentioned, the major objection which is frequently raised against the whole exercise is that it may lead to more, and particularly more detailed, public intervention in the private sector of the economy. The government may be hard put to resist the temptation to "correct" imbalances that show up in the forecast. Strong political forces, as well as the pressure of private interest groups, may push in that direction. In the opinion of the critics, this would tend to undermine the private enterprise system by shifting private responsibilities to the government and would on balance lead to reduced economic efficiency. The doubtful gains in terms of structural balance would be more than offset by a loss of incentives and a loss of flexibility.

These objections were voiced in the EEC context particularly by Germany. Opinions clashed in a famous debate in the European

Parliament between Erhard, at that time German Minister of Economic Affairs and a prominent exponent of the "soziale Marktwirtschaft," and Hallstein, President of the European Commission of the EEC. The occasion was a debate on the European Commission's Action Program for the Second Stage of the EEC, in which the Commission first announced its intention to institute some form of common "programming" on the Community level. The basic objections were well summarized by Erhard: "I have never met with a planning administration which has not been animated, in all honesty of will, by a desire to see its plans realized. Because every man has faith in his work and is convinced of its necessity and utility; otherwise all would be illusion and fraud." In other words, projections tend to be transformed into targets, and this in turn will lead governments to take whatever measures are required to see that the targets are realized. The dubious gains from such measures are obtained at the price of a potentially quite serious loss of the efficiency and flexibility of the private enterprise system.

As a matter of fact, the French government has used rather specific, selective instruments to induce shifts in the pattern of private investment: selective tax incentives, selective credit facilities, control over access to the capital market, etc. In addition, the public authorities directly control the approximately 40 per cent of total investment which is carried out by the government itself and by local authorities and nationalized industries.

It is sometimes said that the selective instruments are used to "force compliance with the plan." This is misleading, as practically every black-or-white statement in this grey area is misleading. It is certainly wrong if used in connection with the measures that are incorporated in the plan. Such preannounced government measures are not used to induce compliance with "the" plan, but to change the outcome of the market mechanism from what it would have been without the government measures. This is registered in the plan, but it does not make the plan itself into a detailed target, imposed on the entire economy by public decision. To a large extent, the plan still remains a forecast, which incorporates a number of government measures. Of course, the more prevalent these types of selective measures, the closer the plan does come to a detailed target for the economy as a whole. But it would be highly exaggerated to say that the French practice is anywhere near this situation. Also, one should not disregard the other side of the ledger: in some cases the selective policies incorporated in the plan replace ad hoc protective measures that might otherwise have been taken at a later date, when the industry concerned would have got into the difficulties which the structural measures under discussion are designed to prevent.

The matter is somewhat different for selective measures that are not incorporated in the plan but are taken during the planning period with the purpose of preventing deviations from the projection. Such measures do have the implication of "forcing compliance with the plan," and they pose a far greater threat to the competitive market system than preannounced measures. This target orientation of the plan with respect to developments in the private sector is far stronger in France than it is in the Netherlands. The French plan, for example, is submitted for formal approval to Parliament, whereas the Dutch forecast is simply submitted for information. The former procedure obviously implies a stronger commitment to the plan than the latter. A more important difference is that the Dutch forecasts are revolving, which de-emphasizes their target orientation, whereas the French plans cover continuous four-year periods. At the insistence of the Dutch delegation, this feature of a revolving forecast has been incorporated in the planning framework of the European Economic Community.

The possible target orientation of the plan and its implications for policy bring me to a second major objection that is frequently levied against the planning technique: its supposed tendency to induce policies which attempt to shield the economy against unforeseen disturbances, particularly those arising from international trade. It is true that the French economy has been traditionally protectionistic, but this circumstance surely cannot be blamed on the planning technique, since it far antedates any attempts at national planning. It is also true that any technique can be abused, but this is not sufficient grounds for indicting it. The fact of the matter is that the medium-term planning framework may indeed be used as a tool of national protection, but it may also serve as a weapon *against* protectionist tendencies. In fact, a good case can be made for the proposition that the planning framework may on balance have an antiprotectionist bias. By making the long-term relationship between exports and imports explicit, it may be used to strengthen the otherwise rather weak countervailing power of export interests against the pressures of protection-minded groups. Moreover, medium-term policy tends to favor structural adjustments and policies to aid adaptation rather than ad hoc protectionist measures. Such structural policies are politically more palatable in a medium-term framework because they are more credible than they are without the long-run perspective that shows the alternatives and the opportunities for adjustment offered by a growing economy.

The recent tendency in French policies and planning has been towards greater flexibility and more emphasis on competition, both nationally and internationally. There is no doubt that the opening up of the French economy to unfettered competition in the Common Market has been largely responsible for this development. But it does not at all imply the bankruptcy of the medium-term planning technique. It has changed the policy content without destroying its major objectives: providing improved information to business and government, and inducing more effective coordination and planning of public policy in the framework of a medium-term development perspective for the entire economy.

A well-founded and meaningful evaluation of medium-term economic policy in a national planning framework is difficult, if not impossible, to make. For one thing, serious complications arise in interpreting what evidence there is. Many countries, Germany in particular, have grown as fast as or faster than France without engaging in any national medium-term planning at all, and many have grown at a slower rate. Moreover, the French experience is not necessarily indicative, because the economic structure and history of individual countries are so different. Compare, for example, the stagnation of the French economy before World War II with the buoyant prewar economy of Germany, or the cartelized industrial structure and generally conservative practices in Europe with the growth-oriented outlook of American business.

In a more fundamental sense, the final evaluation hinges on two questions of judgment. First, to what extent does the planning framework induce additional, selective, and detailed intervention in the private sector of the economy, rather than serving only to rationalize existing public policies? Second, how harmful is increased selective intervention in private business decisions? If the answer to the first question is largely negative, one can unambiguously state that the planning framework is a valuable tool for rationalizing economic policy, both short- and medium-term. It serves (a) to emphasize structural as against ad hoc policies, the latter often relying on too strong a dosage (of the stop-go type) or on protectionistic and conservative-oriented measures, in both internal and international economic policy; (b) to rationalize public policy by enforcing internal consistency of the policies pursued by the different units of authority within the public sector; and (c) to improve the adjustment of public policy to developments in the economy as a whole. On the other hand, if and to the extent that the planning framework does induce more, and more detailed, intervention in the private sector, its evaluation becomes more controversial, since it then raises all the issues that concern the very basis of our economic order. Whether as a matter of practical policy the latter element, the possible interventionist tendency, can be separated from the former, the pure rationalization of economic policy, is one of the difficult questions in this area, to which neither experience nor general considerations have so far been able to provide an answer.

Planning for Growth in the Community

I would now like to pass on to the endeavors of the European Economic Community in the area of planning for growth. Understandably, the main pressure toward Community planning has come from France, which saw its national planning efforts being threatened by the establishment of the Common Market. The lowering of trade barriers in the Community meant that foreign trade took up an increasing part of GNP, which could no longer be included in the national forecasting framework or subjected to direct influence by the public authorities. As I have mentioned before, this induced a greater flexibility in French planning as well as an increased emphasis on competition within the French economy and on competitiveness towards the outside, but it also quite naturally led France to push for Community efforts to compensate for the reduced effectiveness of national medium-term forecasting and policy. In recent years, the French position has gained active support from other quarters, in particular from those associated with the European Coal and Steel Community. The long-lasting coal crisis and the more recent difficulties in the steel sector have convinced many that an adequate approach to these problems requires the six countries not just to coordinate their specific policies with respect to coal and steel but to follow a more general approach based on an integrated policy plan for all problems that are in one way or another linked with the specific difficulties of the coal and steel industries. The same holds for other problem areas in which national governments have intervened, such as shipbuilding, textiles, and so on. The logic of the Common Market demands coordination on the Community level, and efficiency in public policy would seem to favor an integrated approach to all these problems rather than separate efforts. Hence the present call for a general "industry policy" for the Community. Last, but certainly not least, it is felt that the coordination of monetary, fiscal, and incomes policies required for short-term stabilization in the Community and for future progress toward currency union can hope to be successful only if it is supported by a common medium-term policy plan that includes these short-term objectives.

What is the "philosophy" of the Rome Treaty, if any, with regard to all these questions? Curiously, the Treaty does not mention medium-term policy at all, and the point did not explicitly come up during the negotiations which led to the Treaty. It is doubtful that anyone at the time, even in the French delegation, consciously envisaged any future activities of the Community in this area. At that time coordination of economic policy was still regarded as necessary and desirable only where it directly served to ensure free trade and to prevent distortions of competition. Wherever this involved certain specific policy areas, as in agriculture and transport, the Treaty explicitly required common policies, or coordination of national policies, both in the short and in the longer run, but an integrated medium-term policy plan for all areas of public responsibility was clearly not envisaged. Consequently, the Treaty does not contain any explicit references to medium-term economic policy. Any initiatives in the area must be based on the very general provision of Article 145, which states that "with a view to ensuring the achievement of the objectives laid down in the Treaty . . . the Council shall ensure the co-ordination of the general economic policies of the Member States."

Starting with its 1962 Action Program, the European Commission has actively advocated Community-wide planning for growth. Its initial proposals seemed to go fairly far in the direction of active public intervention, to be carried out on the basis of a combined economic "plan" for the six countries of the Community. Although it was emphasized that the plan would not be in the nature of a target for the private sector of the economy, the general spirit of the proposal seemed to belie this statement. The Action

Program proposed that if actual developments were to deviate markedly from the plan the Commission would issue appropriate policy recommendations to the member states. It is doubtful whether the Commission and in particular its most directly responsible member, M. Marjolin, really envisaged a detailed public intervention on the basis of the Community plan, but the wording of the proposal shocked some member countries into rather strong initial opposition to the whole effort. The reaction was especially pronounced in Germany, as witnessed by the famous Erhard-Hallstein debate in the European Parliament, to which I referred earlier. Although somewhat less outspoken, the Netherlands were also highly critical of the Commission approach.

Cautioned by this reaction, the Commission in 1963 submitted a formal proposal in which its real or imagined interventionist tendencies were considerably toned down. As subsequently agreed upon with some minor modifications by the Council of National Ministers in 1964, the present Community setup is as follows.

A committee of independent economic experts is charged with the task of making a (disaggregated) projection of medium-term economic development in the Community, on the basis of national projections and of any other information to which it has access. At the insistence of the German delegation, the Ministers decided to instruct the experts to work out several variants of the projection, based on different hypotheses concerning the economic policies to be followed by the public authorities. The report of the committee of experts is submitted to the European Commission, which may add its comments, and to the Council of National Ministers.

A second committee, consisting of senior civil servants of the member countries and of the European Commission, will use this report to set up an economic policy plan for the coming years, reflecting the intentions both of the national governments and of the Community. This policy plan is referred to as the "[medium-term economic policy] *program*," and the corresponding forecast as the "[medium-term economic] *projection.*"

There are various interesting points to be noted with regard to this procedure. One concerns the institutional separation of the projection and the program. This reflects an attempt, on the part of the German delegation in particular, to emphasize that the Community procedure has two separate objectives: (1) providing a medium-term projection for the Community as a whole, which improves upon a simple bundling of national forecasts by bringing in the interrelationships among the member economies as endogenous variables, and (2) rationalizing the medium-term economic policies of national governments and of the Community by integrating them in one policy program. The projection would not in any sense be a plan, as it would contain no targets but only forecasts, a feature emphasized by the inclusion of alternative versions (a German addition to the original proposal) and by the revolving nature of the forecasts (a Dutch addition). The program, on the other hand, would simply register public policy intentions, as modified in accordance with the requirements of policy coordination within the Community, and it would have no implication of increasing the extent of government intervention in the private sector of the economy.

In some respects, the Community procedure is basically different from national planning techniques. The element that is most conspicuously absent is the direct collaboration of business, which plays such an important role in the national "management decision game." The business world participates only in an indirect manner, namely, to the extent that it cooperates in setting up the national projections on which the Community projection is largely based. This absence of direct involvement on the part of business has been a source of criticism against the first activities of the Community in this area, and presumably consultations with management and labor organizations will be included from now on. But it is questionable whether, at least during the foreseeable future, the role of business on the Community level will grow into a more active participation such as is realized nationally. For the time being, it would seem inconceivable that the elaborate technique employed, for example, in the French national planning framework, could be copied on the Community level. On the positive side, this implies that the Community procedure does not raise any threat to competition, such as may arise from the close cooperation of business in the national planning framework.

The main emphasis in the Community procedure is therefore inevitably on the program, which reflects the national policy intentions, the intended policies of the Community, and the attempts at policy coordination on the part of member states. The program raises an interesting question. To what extent do the national administrations and the Community institutions commit themselves to the policy intentions laid down in the program? The text of the decision states that the program should contain "the broad lines of the economic policies intended to be pursued by Member States and institutions of the Community . . . and should aim at ensuring their co-ordination." It goes on to say that "by agreeing to the programme the Council and the governments of the Member States will express their intention to act in accordance with its main concepts." The precise commitments thus made are difficult to define. It is not clear what legal possibilities exist to enforce them. Politically, however, the program, once accepted, does impose a constraint on the freedom of member states, since they would have to justify any deviations from the program in their national political arena as well as in Brussels. No doubt the real content of this constraint will initially be rather weak, since each member state will hesitate to tie down its partners in order not to compromise its own political freedom of action. But the strength of the commitment may grow as the economic and political cohesion of the Community increases.

Last year, the first Community program with accompanying projection, both covering the period 1966-70, was agreed upon. One has the impression that the aspect of active coordination between the partners has been almost totally absent. The policy intentions which it contains are simply a collection of national objectives, supplemented with some rather vague and general recommendations. Obviously, the policy committee that is responsible for this first effort, based as it is on a rather fragile compromise between the divergent politico-economic views of the two major countries of the Community, felt that it had to avoid any appearance of interventionism so as not to endanger the compromise. One of the more interesting aspects of the program, as it finally evolved, is the emphasis on short-term stability as a primary policy objective. It is stated explicitly that "if the projected growth rates are inconsistent with price stability and equilibrium on the balance of payments, difficult policy decisions will have to be made; they should tend towards giving priority to the objective of price stability." This statement shows more clearly than any other indication in the program, such as the absence of detailed interventionist policies, that the countries of the Community intend to put a high priority on maintaining external equilibrium and that in order to achieve this they intend to rely on a sound macroeconomic framework with active competition internally. There is no indication at all of any tendency to induce a forced rate of economic growth, with selective internal policies and protection towards the outside.

But what of the future? It is often said that the EEC does have a general *dirigiste* and protectionist bias, which will become increasingly evident as the Community develops. Supposedly, this general bias would follow in particular from the Community's activities and intentions with regard to medium-term economic policy and planning. Is this judgment justified? Both issues, dirigism and protectionism, are, of course, of quite fundamental importance to the political and economic future of the Common Market. It appears appropriate as well as worth our while to devote the last part of this all too brief review of economic policy and planning in the European Economic Community to a short examination of each of these points.

Does public planning, and in particular the coordination of medium-term planning in the Community, lead to more dirigism? I do not believe that this question lends itself to a meaningful general answer. As I have tried to demonstrate, planning is but a tool which can be used to increase as well as to reduce the scope of detailed public intervention in the economy. In being transferred, at least in part, from the national capitals to Brussels, the tool gains power in one respect and loses it in another. It gains because the Community as a whole is less dependent on the outside than are the individual countries, and this tends to increase the degree of freedom in economic policy. It loses power because the added difficulties of formulating and effectuating economic measures on the Community level impede the possibility of detailed intervention. In fact, the political left has often raised as a criticism of the Common Market the weakening of economic policy that results from its being transferred from the relatively strong national administrations to the still rather tenuous power center in Brussels. The idea of a very strong, highly centralized, and interventionist-oriented Community surely seems extremely naive, considering present political reality. The danger is rather that the Community will be too weak in dealing with structural problems, as was clearly evidenced by the coal crisis and the inability of the Community to provide a common solution. This weakness not only threatens the Common Market itself by inducing countries to revert to national measures; it also invites private cartel agreements to do the job instead.

But these comments concern only the immediate potential. Whether in the more distant future the actual policies of the Community will on balance be more or less *dirigiste* than the national policies which they replace will depend on the evolution of the political climate and on the shifting balance of power in the Community as it is affected by the possible admission of new members, among other things. If one simply extrapolates current developments, two tendencies emerge. One is that political views in the six countries are definitely converging. Whereas France has moved to a greater emphasis on flexibility and competition, Germany has begun to realize the advantages of integrated medium-term policy plans, and the Netherlands have set up their own planning framework. This is one of the more interesting examples of the learning process that goes on in the Community. Considering the violent antagonism of Germany and the somewhat less violent reservations of the Netherlands in the period after the European Commission first announced its intention of moving to some form of "programming" on the Community level, the convergence of views is indeed remarkable. The other tendency is the bias in this process toward less, as well as less detailed, intervention in the Community as a whole. The increased reliance of France on competition has not been offset to any significant extent by a departure from the guiding concept of the "soziale Marktwirtschaft" in Germany.

Finally, what about the alleged protectionistic tendencies which comprehensive policy planning would impose upon the Community? I have attempted to show that planning as such need not have any such bias, indeed that it may well serve to reduce protection by mobilizing export interests as a countervailing power and by putting increased emphasis on structural adjustments rather than on the inefficient palliative of protection. It is perhaps something of a paradox that these potential advantages can be realized only with a strong decision-making process in the Community. A weak federal executive will be unable to provide the positive policies for growth and structural adaptation which can serve as viable alternatives to protection in the case of difficulties in any particular sector of the economy. Protection is politically often the easy way out because, at least in the short run, it puts part of the burden of adjustment on the outside suppliers, who have no vote at all and who hold no power other than the very indirect one of retaliation. A weak federal executive will be hard put to resist the pressures towards protection, faced as it is with the threat of unilateral action by producer countries in the Community, and tempted by the relative ease of bribing net importing countries into agreeing to common measures of protection. Moreover, lack of common action may force the executive tacitly to authorize private cartels to take over where it cannot itself effectively provide the necessary support for structural adaptation.

This brings me back full circle to the theme of my first chapter: the vital role which a strong, decision-making process of the federal type plays in shaping the future of the European Economic Community. It is not only an essential precondition for the survival of the Community and for its future development toward a real economic union; it will also be a very important factor if the Community is to be open and dynamic in its external policies, thus averting the danger of immobilism and regional isolationism on the eastern side of the Atlantic that might result from a weak political structure. Such a development would be a tragedy for the entire world economy. In the coming years all our hopes and efforts must be directed at building a strong Community of Europe, since only a strong Community can be a true partner in the very real bonds of head and heart that link our continents.